baje
3/11

Animals Working Together

Ants and Aphids Work Together

by Martha E. H. Rustad

Consulting Editor: Gail Saunders-Smith, PhD

Consultant: Jackie Gai, DVM
Zoo and Exotic Animal Consultation

CAPSTONE PRESS
a capstone imprint

Pebble Plus is published by Capstone Press,
151 Good Counsel Drive, P.O. Box 669, Mankato, Minnesota 56002.
www.capstonepub.com

Books published by Capstone Press are manufactured with paper
containing at least 10 percent post-consumer waste.

Library of Congress Cataloging-in-Publication Data
Rustad, Martha E. H. (Martha Elizabeth Hillman), 1975–
  Ants and aphids work together / by Martha E. H. Rustad.
     p. cm.—(Pebble plus. Animals working together)
  Includes bibliographical references and index.
  Summary: "Simple text and full-color photographs introduces the symbiotic relationship of ants and aphids"—Provided
by publisher.
  ISBN 978-1-4296-5298-8 (library binding)
  ISBN 978-1-4296-6197-3 (paperback)
  1. Ants—Ecology—Juvenile literature. 2. Aphids—Ecology—Juvenile literature. 3. Symbiosis—Juvenile literature. I.
Title. II. Series.
  QL568.F7R87 2011
  595.79'61785—dc22   2010025460

Editorial Credits
Erika L. Shores, editor; Bobbie Nuytten, designer; Svetlana Zhurkin, media researcher;
    Laura Manthe, production specialist

Photo Credits
Alamy/Ant Life/Antje Schulte, 12–13; Nigel Cattlin, 17; WoodyStock, 4–5
Minden Pictures/Konrad Wothe, cover, 18–19
Photolibrary/François Gilson, 6–7
Shutterstock/Bruce MacQueen, 1, 9; Mark William Penny, 21; pixelman, 11
Visuals Unlimited/Alex Wild, 15

Note to Parents and Teachers

The Animals Working Together series supports national science standards related to biology.
This book describes and illustrates the relationship between ants and aphids. The images
support early readers in understanding the text. The repetition of words and phrases helps early
readers learn new words. This book also introduces early readers to subject-specific vocabulary
words, which are defined in the Glossary section. Early readers may need assistance to read
some words and to use the Table of Contents, Glossary, Read More, Internet Sites, and Index
sections of the book.

Printed in the United States of America in North Mankato, Minnesota.
092010
005933CGS11

Table of Contents

Symbiosis

In a forest, aphids scurry

down a plant.

A hungry ant waits nearby.

It quickly picks up an aphid.

Is the aphid in danger?

No, the aphid is safe.

Ants do not eat aphids.

Ants drink a sweet liquid

made by aphids.

Ants and aphids are partners.
Together they find food, shelter,
and safety. This relationship
is called symbiosis.

Aphids Help Ants

Aphids suck juices from plants.

They eat more than they need.

Aphid bodies put out the extra juices. The liquid is called honeydew. Ants rub aphids' bodies. Ants drink the honeydew that comes out.

Ants Help Aphids

Aphids sometimes suck
all the juices from a plant.
The plant dies. Aphids need
a new plant to eat. Ants carry
aphids to new plants.

Ants keep aphids safe. Ants bite ladybugs and other predators and chase them away. Ants sometimes even eat ladybug eggs.

Ants let aphids live in their colonies. Ants even keep aphid eggs safe during winter. Ants guard the colony to keep out predators.

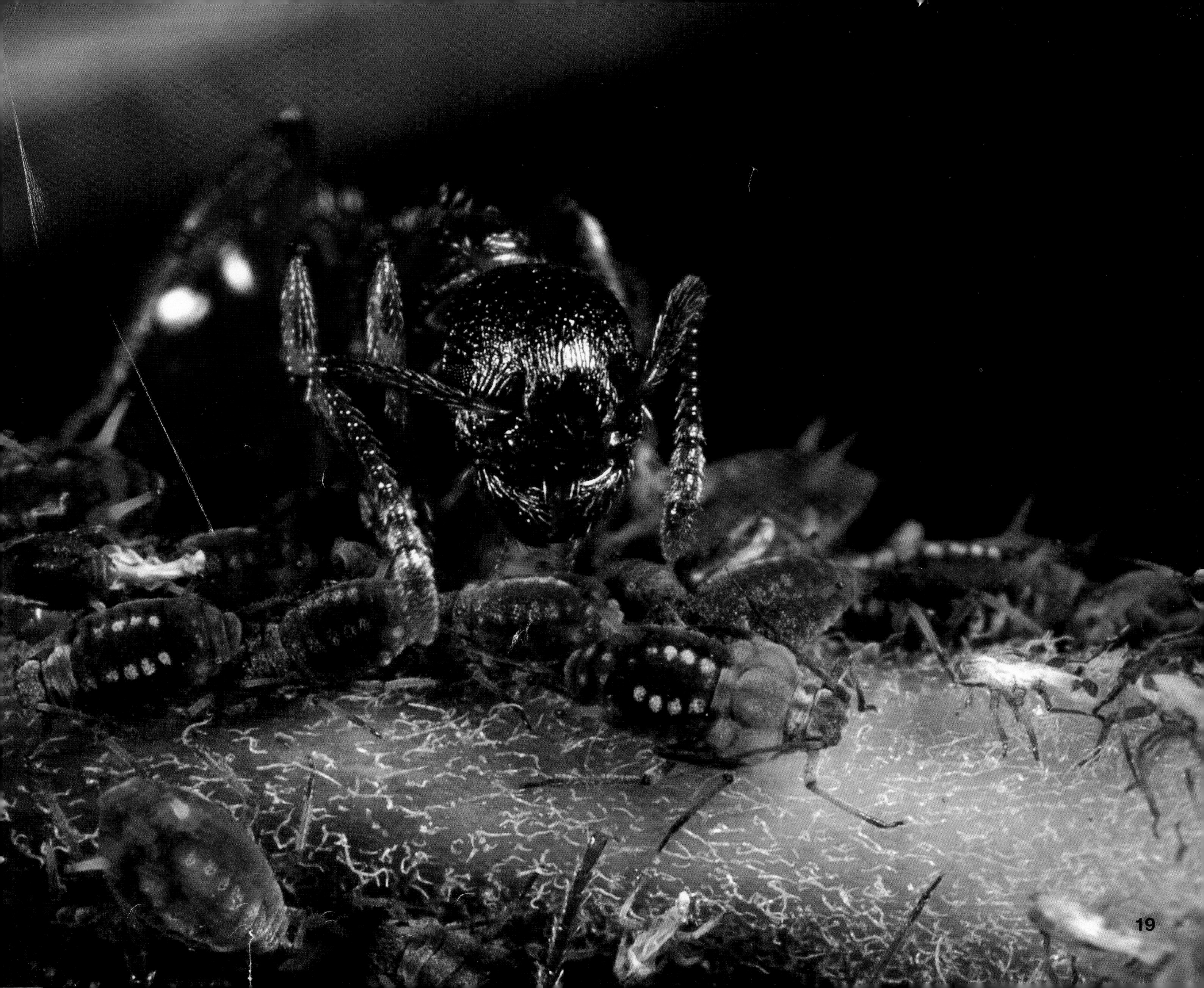

Teamwork

In a busy forest, ants and
aphids are a team.
Symbiosis keeps both animals
healthy and safe.

21

Glossary

colony—a large group of animals that live together

guard—to watch over and protect

honeydew—a sweet liquid made inside the bodies of aphids

predator—an animal that hunts and eats another animal; aphid predators include ladybugs and lacewings

scurry—to move along quickly

symbiosis—a relationship between two different kinds of animals; the animals live together to help each other find food, shelter, or safety

Read More

Aronin, Miriam. *The Ant's Nest: A Huge, Underground City.* Spectacular Animal Towns. New York: Bearport Pub., 2010.

Sexton, Colleen A. *Aphids.* World of Insects. Minneapolis: Bellwether Media, 2009.

Silverman, Buffy. *You Scratch My Back.* Raintree Fusion. Chicago: Raintree, 2008.

Internet Sites

FactHound offers a safe, fun way to find Internet sites related to this book. All of the sites on FactHound have been researched by our staff.

Here's all you do:

Visit *www.facthound.com*

Type in this code: 9781429652988

Super-cool stuff! Check out projects, games and lots more at www.capstonekids.com

Index

Word Count: 178
Grade: 1
Early-Intervention Level: 17